THE LAYOVER

THE LAYOVER

Devotionals For When You're Between Where
You Were and Where You're Going

RONICE FELICIA LATTA

Trilogy Christian Publishers

A Wholly Owned Subsidiary of Trinity Broadcasting Network

2442 Michelle Drive

Tustin, CA 92780

For information, address Trilogy Christian Publishing

Rights Department, 2442 Michelle Drive, Tustin, Ca 92780.

Trilogy Christian Publishing/TBN and colophon are trademarks of Trinity Broadcasting Network.

For information about special discounts for bulk purchases, please contact Trilogy Christian Publishing.

Manufactured in the United States of America

10 9 8 7 6 5 4 3 2 1

Library of Congress Cataloging-in-Publication Data is available.

ISBN 978-1-64088-597-4

ISBN 978-1-64088-598-1 (ebook)

DEDICATION

Dedicated to my wonderful husband, son, and daughter.

I am grateful for your motivation and support. You are gifts from God, and I love you all.

INTRODUCTION

This book was initially written out of personal frustration as I walked with God during a very difficult season of loss. I was bound by disappointment, stuck on a lonely road between where I used to be and where I was being called to. What started as periodic journaling quickly turned into a collection of devotional writings.

Documenting my journey got me through the agonizing moments when my mind and heart were at complete odds. Writing offered the temporary relief that I desperately needed. It was the glue that held my broken pieces together. It gave me purpose. It gave me vision. It gave me hope.

These devotionals are intended to encourage those who struggle with loss that has occurred unexpectedly or unnecessarily, due to no fault of their own. Such losses are usually the result of the physical death of someone precious, or the natural end of something dear. In my particular case, loss came in the form of a layoff from a world-renowned company that I'd been a part of for almost three decades.

Sometimes the aftermath of loss is so devastating that it can cause us to lose our way. Therefore, how we choose to push past the pain is of the utmost importance. Fervent prayer helped me to navigate the waves of grief. Restoration would eventually come, but in the meantime, I had to figure out how to move towards my destiny. I refer to this interim period as *"the layover,"* because I was forced to wait (for what felt like forever) on a divine connection in an uncomfortable and unfamiliar space. It wasn't obvious at the time, but it is now. God, in His great mercy, allotted me time to reconcile my loss with His sovereignty. It was a long and arduous task, but He brought me safely through.

I wouldn't take anything for my journey now. For what I have gained in Christ has far outweighed what I have lost. I have learned how to completely lean and depend on Jesus. Now it's my sincere prayer to inspire others to do the same.

TABLE OF CONTENTS

COUNT YOUR BLESSINGS

"Because of the Lord's great love we are not consumed, for his compassions never fail" (Lamentations 3:22 NIV).

Overcome with joy as they stood watching the annual ball drop in New York's Times Square, twelve-year old Jack exclaimed, "Mom, you are the reason my life is so wonderful!" The words filled Stacy's heart with forever love. This was just one of many special moments the two had shared, but they were not all as exciting as this one.

Life is filled with ups and downs. In the course of a year, we may celebrate happy occasions like the birth of a grandchild or the marriage of a dear friend. We may also experience difficult circumstances, such as the death of a loved one or the loss of a job. Whatever the case, it's best to focus on our blessings, not our shortfalls.

"Great is Thy Faithfulness," a popular Christian hymn, reminds us that our heavenly Father remains faithful day in and day out, in the best and worst of times. His love for us is displayed in so many wonderful ways in each new day, in every New Year.

Lord, thank You for Your goodness. All that we need, Your hands provide.

MORNING BY MORNING, NEW MERCIES WE SEE.

THE RETURN

"I will set out and go back to my father and say to him: Father, I have sinned against heaven and against you" (Luke 15:18 NIV).

Overwhelmed by ongoing problems, I finally sought the scriptures for help. Fear and doubt had me feeling empty and alone. Perhaps you've been there? Why do we wait so long to go to God? It would behoove us to come to our senses quicker.

We can learn a valuable lesson from the Prodigal Son in Luke 15. In this parable, Jesus speaks of a wayward son who squandered his inheritance. Then, in despair, he returned home to beg his father's forgiveness. The father graciously welcomed him back with open arms.

Life has a way of presenting challenging situations that could cause us to lose our way. Some problems we can't control, but some we bring upon ourselves. In either case, this message is here to remind us of God's redemptive grace and everlasting love. If you are feeling lost, follow the example of the son and run back to your heavenly Father. Boldly confess your need for Him. He is patiently waiting for you.

Dear Lord, help us to remember that we are never alone, because You are always with us.

THERE'S NO PLACE LIKE HOME.

JUST ASK

"Don't worry about anything; instead, pray about everything.
Tell God what you need, and thank him for all he has done"
(Philippians 4:6 NLT).

As five-year old Nia knelt down, she decided that tonight's bedtime prayer would include one very special request: "God, please tell Mommy and Daddy to take me to Disney World. Thank you. Amen." Her prior pleas had seemingly fallen on deaf ears, but surely they'd listen to Him, she thought. Little did she know that her parents had been secretly planning her dream vacation for quite a while. A few weeks later, to her joyful surprise, the family stood in front of the Cinderella Castle at Magic Kingdom!

We adults are no different than this precious child. We try to do things in our own strength and power. Then, after many failed attempts, we finally petition God for what He already intended to give us. Little did we know that He was just waiting for us to ask.

The Apostle Paul urged the church at Philippi to go to God for everything, big and small. He learned firsthand, through many trials and tribulations, that God would supply their every need. The same is true for all believers, today and forevermore.

Like any loving parent, our heavenly Father delights in giving us our heart's desire. Trusting Him must be our first priority, though, not our last resort.

Lord, You know my wants and needs even before I ask.
Therefore, help me to align my will with Yours.

WHILE WE'RE TRYING TO FIGURE IT OUT, GOD
HAS ALREADY WORKED IT OUT!

TRUST
GOD'S TIMING

"Take delight in the Lord, and he will give you the desires of your heart. Commit your way to the Lord; trust in him and he will do this: He will make your righteous reward shine like the dawn, your vindication like the noonday sun. Be still before the Lord and wait patiently for him" (Psalm 37:4-7a NIV).

We live in a microwave society. We want everything to happen quickly. We see it now; we want it now. Technological advancements, while mostly beneficial, also come with consequential side effects. Our attention spans have shortened, and we find our patience dwindling too—not only with one another, but even with God.

"When are You going to bless me? I need You now!" In the middle of a painfully long transition period, I desperately pleaded with God for instant relief. My unexpected job loss had led to other unforeseen circumstances. Nothing was going right. My prayers went seemingly unanswered.

At my breaking point, God spoke to me in a discernable voice. I clearly heard Him say, *"A cake must be baked for a specific amount of time for it to come out perfectly. If you increase the temperature in an effort to decrease the baking time, then it won't cook from within. You'll end up with a burnt, collapsed cake that's not fit to eat. The same is true for you. You won't receive all that I have in store for you if this process is rushed. You won't be healed from the inside out. Daughter, this season must run its course for you to come out whole."*

Everything doesn't work according to our timetable. Things will happen at the appointed time. Don't try to force a situation. Keep honoring and trusting God. That husband, that wife, that baby, that house, that job—that "thing" you're waiting for—is on the way! Going through the process may not be a "piece of cake," but if you endure until the end, the outcome will be just as sweet.

*Heavenly Father, nothing catches You by surprise. You
know the beginning, the middle, and the end of my story.
Help me to patiently go through the process.*

YOU CAN'T HURRY GOD. YOU HAVE TO WAIT.

STORMS OF LIFE

"When Jesus woke up, he rebuked the wind and said to the waves, 'Silence! Be still!' Suddenly the wind stopped, and there was a great calm" (Mark 4:39 NLT).

Hurricane Harvey made landfall in Houston, Texas on August 25, 2017. What began as an ordinary storm quickly intensified into an extraordinary hurricane that resulted in catastrophic flooding and tragic loss. Over 100 people perished. The count would have been larger, but fortunately, residents heeded early warnings.

Similarly, in everyday life, unpredicted crises have a way of rising up out of the blue. When we least expect it, troubling news may come in the form of an undiagnosed illness, uninvited layoff, or unwanted breakup. Challenging times are simply a part of life. At some point, something we are not expecting will happen. In fact, I once heard it put this way: we're either entering a storm, going through a storm, or coming out of a storm.

One of the best known gospel stories is that of Jesus calming the raging sea. Jesus, who had been asleep, was awakened by His terrified disciples. A fierce storm caused them to fear for their lives. They thought they were going to drown, so they cried out to Him for help. Jesus quickly got the situation under control with one resounding command, "Peace, be still!"

This biblical account is here to serve as a vivid reminder for us to not lose heart during times of difficulty. We can find comfort in knowing that Jesus is with us. Surely, if He can make howling winds cease and flood waters retreat, then He can silence the personal storms that come our way.

Lord Jesus, You're the Captain of my soul. Thank You for helping me to weather the storms of life. I stand in awe of Your mighty power. I will forever praise Your holy name!

IF I NEVER HAD PROBLEMS, I WOULDN'T KNOW
JESUS COULD SOLVE THEM.

LOOK UP

"I will lift up mine eyes unto the hills, from whence cometh my help. My help cometh from the Lord, which made heaven and earth" (Psalm 121:1-2 KJV).

One day I was having trouble finding a particular item at the grocery store. Knowing I was in the correct aisle and section, I kept searching. I looked forward, down, and around, but still couldn't find what I was looking for. Just when I was about to give up, I looked up. Lo and behold, the item was sitting in plain sight on the top shelf!

Similar scenarios occurred again and again. Finally, it dawned on me—God was trying to teach me a valuable lesson: when I can't find what I'm looking for down here, I should look up to Him for help. What I'd been experiencing in the natural was affirmed in my spirit, and confirmed by Psalm 121. "I will lift up my eyes to the hills, from whence cometh my help. My help comes from the Lord." The author of this Psalm presents a clear picture of God as our ever-present helper and keeper.

Our caring, wise God helps us to find profound significance even in the mundane. When we look up, the One who made heaven and earth will demonstrate His love for us in unexpected places, in unexpected ways.

Dear Lord, we look up to You with a steadfast hope, for we know our help comes from above.

VICTORY IS CONNECTED TO US LOOKING UP TO GOD, NOT AROUND TO OTHERS.

REFLECTIONS

"All the people we saw were huge. We even saw giants there, the descendants of Anak. Next to them we felt like grasshoppers, and that's what they thought, too!" (Numbers 13:32b-33 NLT).

What do you see when you look in the mirror? Do you liken yourself to a cat—a small, timid, playful creature, or to a lion—a big, strong, stately being? Sometimes we view ourselves through the lens of someone else. In other words, we entertain and believe the negative opinions of others. Or we make the mistake of drawing comparisons. In so doing, we are left feeling inadequate and insignificant.

This was the case when Moses, as commanded by God, sent out twelve tribal leaders of Israel to explore the land of Canaan. The Lord had already promised to give the Israelites the "land flowing with milk and honey." They just had to go in and take it. But fear, doubt, and unbelief prevented them from possessing the land. Ultimately, Caleb and Joshua were the only ones rewarded for taking God at His Word. Because they had different attitudes than the others, they were allowed to enter the Promised Land.

You don't have to be the most skilled, the most talented, the most intelligent, or the most beautiful to exude confidence. You can silence the naysayers simply by knowing who you are and whose you are. You are a child of God, created in His image (Genesis 1:26-27, Ephesians 1:11, Ephesians 2:10, Ephesians 3:12). Therefore, reflect the likeness of your heavenly Father.

Begin each day anew with a faith-filled attitude. Start by believing what God says about you, and remember this: most people see you the way you see yourself. So even when you feel like a cat, act like a lion!

Dear Lord, help us to see ourselves through Your eyes. Clothe us in confidence and empower us with Your Holy Spirit. Help us to not be impressed by people, but rather to be inspired by Your Word.

YOUR ATTITUDE DETERMINES YOUR ALTITUDE.

HIGH
IMPACT WORKOUT

"Keep yourself in training for a godly life. Physical exercise has some value, but spiritual exercise is valuable in every way, because it promises life both for the present and for the future" (1 Timothy 4:7b-8 GNT).

Legendary fitness expert Jack LaLanne taught the health benefits of regular exercise and a wholesome diet. He believed, "You eat every day, you sleep every day, and your body was made to exercise every day." While some may view this philosophy as fanatical, no one can refute the point that movement is good for the body—and the benefits extend beyond the physical. Medical studies show that vigorous exercise triggers the release of euphoric-type brain chemicals called endorphins. These "happy hormones" are why we feel better after a great workout.

Healthy living is also promoted throughout God's Word. "Do you not know that your bodies are temples of the Holy Spirit, who is in you, whom you have received from God?" (1 Corinthians 6:19-20a NIV). "For physical training is of some value, but godliness has value for all things, holding promise for both the present life and the life to come" (1 Timothy 4:8 NIV). The Apostle John also stressed the importance of physical and spiritual strength (3 John 1:2).

The benefits of being spiritually fit are immeasurable, and the ways to do it are innumerable. Here are a few suggestions: to increase your faith, take a daily walk through the Scriptures, for it is all "God-breathed and is useful for teaching, rebuking, correcting and training in righteousness, so that the servant of God may be thoroughly equipped for every good work" (2 Timothy 3:16 NIV); to elevate your mood, listen to inspirational music; and to build character, exercise self-control.

There are many things in this world we can't change, but one thing is for sure: we all have the power to change ourselves. You don't have to be a health guru to recognize the benefits of a proper diet. And you certainly don't have to be a Bible scholar to know that God desires wholeness in His people. My friend, if you're lacking in any area today, commit to becoming a healthier, happier, and more spiritual you. You'll feel better, look better, and inspire others, too!

Lord, we are beautifully and masterfully made. Help us to care for our temples in ways that are pleasing to You. Remove our unhealthy thoughts and filthy habits, so that we may better honor You.

ON YOUR MARK, GET SET, LET'S GO!

FILL ME UP, GOD

"You will keep in perfect peace all who trust in you, all whose thoughts are fixed on you!" (Isaiah 26:3 NLT).

My jeep was on "E," so I pulled into a gas station and instructed the attendant to fill it up. I wonder if this is what we do every Sunday—treat the church like a filling station. Show up and wait for the pastor and the choir to "fill" us up. "Preach until I feel good, and sing me happy!" Sometimes we leave feeling exhilarated, but oftentimes, just as we came—empty.

We fail to realize that the battlefield is in our mind. In order to live a victorious life, we must learn to bring into captivity every thought and make it obedient to Christ (2 Corinthians 10:5). In other words, stop relying on the flesh, and start depending on the Spirit. Developing a relationship with Christ takes time, effort, and commitment. Discerning the Spirit requires contemplation, remediation, and meditation.

When the cares of this world start to drain you, fill up on the promises of God. Encourage yourself throughout the day, every day. Your thoughts will begin to take on a new form, because you will no longer be at the mercy of your impulsive thinking.

Yes, the church is supposed to be a safe haven, where those oppressed and depressed can go to be comforted and revived. However, believers need to also bring in something—a joyful heart, a song of praise—anything that expresses your desire and pleasure to be there. When you come ready for worship, you will not only leave full, but also empowered for the warfare outside the church walls.

Lord God, we are thankful for our places of worship. Please renew our spirits whenever and wherever we assemble. Help us to be mindful that we are not there just for ourselves, but for our brothers and sisters in Christ, too.

YOU GET OUT WHAT YOU PUT IN.

MAKE A JOYFUL NOISE

"Shout with joy to the Lord, all the earth! Worship the Lord with gladness. Come before him, singing with joy" (Psalm 100:1-2 NLT).

While scanning the pews during a church service, I couldn't help but notice how many people were listlessly singing the congregational hymns. Apparently, the pastor realized it too, for he promptly addressed the matter with one reprimanding question, "Is God not worthy to be praised?"

Even when things are going wrong in our lives, we can still rejoice in the Lord. Our worship should always reflect our love and adoration for Him. A half-hearted, robotic demonstration does very little to glorify His name. However, authentic praise flowing from a grateful heart blesses Him—and those around us, too.

So, the next time you assemble for worship, remember that the choir is not the only one charged with making a joyful noise. We're all called to "enter his gates with thanksgiving and his courts with praise; give thanks to him and praise his name" (Psalm 100:4 NIV). Don't hold back on God, for He is certainly worthy to be praised!

Dear Lord, please forgive us when we don't offer the praise You so richly deserve. From now on, we will bless Your name at all times, because You are good!

WHEN PRAISES GO UP, BLESSINGS COME DOWN.

DADDY'S GIRL

"I will not leave you as orphans; I will come to you" (John 14:18 NIV).

As a young child, my daughter required my undivided attention. She was happy as long as I was near. Of course, I understood why—she was a mama's girl!

Great comfort accompanies the presence of unconditional love. I know this from my own relationship with my heavenly Father. When I feel invisible, He sees me. When I feel uncelebrated, He cheers for me. When I feel rejected, He receives me. When I feel like an outsider, He draws me nearer. He's there for me in ways no one else could ever be.

Having the love and support of family is important, but knowing that God is everything we need is essential to our spiritual maturity. Unfortunately, most of us don't rely on this divine truth enough.

Daddy God, I'm so thankful that You know what I need, when I need it, and how I need it. I'm so glad I can always count on You to be there for me.

JESUS SITS HIGH, BUT LOOKS LOW.

SEASONS OF UNCERTAINTY

"Trust in the Lord with all your heart; do not depend on your own understanding. Seek his will in all you do, and he will show you which path to take" (Proverbs 3:5-6 NLT).

I was in unfamiliar territory, on my way to an event, when the signal was lost. All of a sudden, my car's GPS stalled. I continued driving, uncertain if I was still heading in the right direction. In a few seconds, it recalibrated and began directing again. I breathed a sigh of relief. I was back on track.

Most of us experience these moments, and not just on the road. There are times in life when we need guidance, because we're unsure about how to move forward. Times when pressing decisions have to be made, but we don't know what to do. These seasons of uncertainty are often triggered by major life events like a sudden death, a job loss, or maybe a natural disaster.

People handle difficult circumstances differently, but the feelings of anxiety, loneliness, and lostness hit us all at some point. That's usually when we really start searching for God. Where is He? Why won't He answer? Didn't He say, "Never will I leave you; never will I forsake you" (Hebrews 13:5b NIV)? Why then do we feel so alone during these precarious moments? Well, it might take a while to register, but eventually we realize He's there, silently waiting on us. To stop and breathe. To reflect on our situation. To adjust our attitude. To acknowledge that we don't know everything. To relinquish control. To change our perspective. To meditate on His eternal, living Word. To seek His good and perfect will for our lives.

Moving through these long, dry spells is never easy, but those who stay in faith are rewarded. We get to experience God in extraordinary new ways. We are awakened to His amazing grace. We learn to trust Him with reckless abandon. The most profound example of these powerful truths was displayed on the Mount of Olives by our Lord and Savior, Jesus Christ, when He cried out, "Father, if you are willing, take this cup from me; yet not my will, but yours be done" (Luke 22:42 NIV).

In this life, we are bound to have moments of anguish, but know this—trouble don't last always! Clarity, comfort, strength, and peace come to those who place their trust in the Lord. Humble yourself and submit your will to His. His mercy will see you through. And should you veer off course, your internal navigator, the Holy Spirit, will kick in and lead you safely to your divine destination.

Speak, Lord, for Your children are listening. Help us to obey and trust You, even when we don't understand. Amen.

THE SAFEST PLACE TO BE IS IN THE WILL OF GOD.

AUTHENTICALLY ME

"I praise you because I am fearfully and wonderfully made; your works are wonderful, I know that full well" (Psalm 139:14 NIV).

It's hard to admit, but sometimes I feel inadequate. A series of rejections left me doubting my abilities and even wondering how much I mattered. I began to think something was wrong with me. After sharing my insecurities with a trusted friend, I discovered that I'm not alone. She confessed to experiencing similar feelings from time to time.

No matter what, who we are is enough for God. We must accept ourselves for who we are and never try to be someone else. That said, if there is an area which we know requires change, then we should pray about it. The Holy Spirit will correct and prune as needed. Remember, Jesus died for our sins. While we were yet sinners, He died for us (Romans 5:8). There are things God knows about us that we don't even know, yet He loves us anyway!

God wants the best for us. He wants our faith to give us courage and confidence. So we must stop wasting time and energy worrying about things we can't control. Instead, recognize that everything He calls us to do, He also equips us to do through His power.

Dear Lord, thanks for making us a part of Your workmanship.
Help us to be all that You created us to be.

WE ARE UNIQUELY MADE, WITH FLAWS AND ALL!

THESE THREE WORDS

"I press on toward the goal to win the prize for which God has called me heavenward in Christ Jesus" (Philippians 3:14 NIV).

Stretch goals can be described as far-reaching expectations that exceed your current capabilities. Such goals are hard to accomplish in our own power, but a collaboration with God will ensure success. Consider the following three words as your winning formula:

Desire: "Those who live according to the flesh have their minds set on what the flesh desires; but those who live in accordance with the Spirit have their minds set on what the Spirit desires" (Romans 8:5 NIV). Seek God first in everything! Align your desires with His Word and His will. Consult the Holy Spirit. An affirmation of "yes" will reside in your peace, or a confirmation of "no" will hover over your indecision.

Focus: "'Come,' he said. Then Peter got down out of the boat, walked on the water and came toward Jesus. But when he saw the wind, he was afraid and, beginning to sink, cried out, 'Lord, save me!'" (Matthew 14:29-30 NIV). As long as Peter kept his focus on Jesus, he was able to walk on water. Yet the moment he took his eyes off of Jesus, he began to sink. Distractions will come, but don't worry about the circumstances around you. Keep your eyes on Jesus as He beckons you.

Finish: "Being confident of this, that he who began a good work in you will carry it on to completion until the day of Christ Jesus" (Philippians 1:6 NIV). Rest in the blessed assurance that God will be with you every step of the way. You will cross the finish line!

The common thread between these words is faith; faith in God, and faith in yourself. Beloved, dare to dream bigger, to dig deeper, and to aim higher in life. The "pressing" is designed to stretch and grow your faith. So move forward with deliberate intent and unwavering conviction. God, with the aid of the Holy Spirit, will help you reach or even surpass your desired goals. If you fight to the finish, the seemingly impossible will manifest into divine victory.

Lord, thank You for making us goal-setters and dream-chasers. We aspire to be everything that You have called us to be!

KEEP YOUR EYES ON THE PRIZE.

PLAY IN THE GRAY

"We can make our plans, but the Lord determines our steps"
(Proverbs 16:9 NLT).

Until a few years ago, the trajectory of my life was pretty much a straight line. Partly because I've always been a planner, and partly because I've never been much of a risk taker. With me, things were either black or white. In other words, I was accustomed to doing things in an orderly manner. For example, as planned, I went directly from high school to college, from college to career, from courting to marriage, and from wife to mom. My formula for success was simple: do my best, and let God do the rest! As a result, my deliberate actions generally meant that things worked out as expected. That is, until the unexpected happened.

A series of unforeseen twists and turns, including unemployment, brought me to a standstill. I found myself buried under an avalanche of grief and disappointment. The uncertainty that followed discolored my outlook on life. My otherwise colorful disposition turned gray. I was held captive by an overactive mind and a fear of the unknown. Having to find a new job, after being with one company for over twenty-six years, was a daunting task. Friends encouraged me to enjoy the time off. Initially, this was easier said than done, but gradually, I learned to trade resistance for resolve. The following gospel truths were key to my transition:

1. *God is sovereign.* My loss didn't catch Him by surprise. He knew what was going to happen and allowed it just the same.

2. *God can be trusted.* Every fragment of my future didn't have to be figured out in my head in order for me to move forward. I just had to follow God's lead.

3. *God never fails.* Man let me down, not God. He never did and never will.

4. *God is perfect.* I had to abandon the impossible standard I had set for myself of wanting to do everything perfectly. The only perfect one is Christ.

These divine acknowledgments relaxed my mind enough so that I could freely meditate on God's promises. Writing, exercising, volunteering, and networking rounded out my new weekly activities. Over time, my propensity for spontaneity and fun increased. To my delight, I emerged with a new sense of satisfaction, adventure, and victory. I had figured out how to "play in the gray"!

The Lord does not require us to change of our own accord. He knows we need His help. This is why He sometimes allows our circumstances to shift us in new directions. In my case, I'd become comfortable with the mundane. Therefore, God in His infinite wisdom stepped in with an unwelcome break that forced me to pivot from my normal, linear path.

Lord, thank you for making me more comfortable with not knowing what's around every corner. My future is in Your hands. I trust You to work things out for my good. I know You can, and I know You will!

DO WHAT YOU CAN, AND TRUST GOD TO DO WHAT YOU CANNOT.

THE PURSUIT

"When she heard about Jesus, she came up behind him in the crowd and touched his cloak, because she thought, 'If I just touch his clothes, I will be healed.' Immediately her bleeding stopped and she felt in her body that she was freed from her suffering" (Mark 5:27-29 NIV).

I was in dire need of a supernatural touch. I was not in a good place; I hadn't been for a while. Everything seemed to be going wrong. Bogged down with feelings of disappointment and resentment, I sought pastoral counsel. Nothing changed. I confided in family and friends. Still, no change. Time passed. Nothing changed but the seasons. When, God, when? Why, God, why?

I searched the scriptures for answers and direction. Clarity came in bits and pieces. Then one day, it all came together with the story about the woman with an issue of blood. For twelve long years she had sought the doctors for help, but they had left her broke and uncured. Her only hope was now found in Jesus, the Great Physician. She knew in her heart that if she got close enough to touch even the hem of His garment, she'd be made whole. With great faith, she pressed her way through the crowd for her healing!

This unnamed woman could have been any one of us. And like her, I had exhausted all of my options. I, too, had to get to Jesus, and if He wasn't coming to me, then I would pursue Him by:

1. Recognizing that He was the only one who could set me free. (This removed my expectations of others.)

2. Making Him my central focus. (This fixed my attention on the problem-solver instead of the problem.)

3. Invoking the power of the Holy Spirit. (This opened my mind and my heart.)

4. Reading the Bible daily. (This strengthened my belief and increased my faith.)

5. Replacing every negative thought with a positive one. (This restored my hope.)

I wasn't instantly delivered from my crisis. Healing came in increments, the closer I got to Jesus. But once I reached Him, peace flooded my soul like a river!

Perhaps you're struggling with a long-term illness, or a problem that's got you down? Faith is the key to your victory. Beloved, be encouraged; don't give up. Pursue God and His plan for your life. Press your way towards Him as if your very life depends on it—because, after all, it really does.

Lord Jesus, thanks for giving us strength to persevere through tough times. Your grace is sufficient. May our struggles and our victories bring glory to Your name!

MAKE YOUR WAY TO JESUS! A MIRACLE MAY BE HIDDEN IN YOUR PAIN.

GOD'S PERSPECTIVE

"Let us examine our ways and test them, and let us return to the Lord" (Lamentations 3:40 NIV).

American comedian and actor Arsenio Hall had a popular talk show segment called "Things That Make You Go Hmmm." He would ponder certain thoughts aloud and invite the audience to take a closer look with him. In unison, everyone would respond with a resounding "hmmm," as if to say, "Wow, I never looked at it that way before!" As I recently examined my personal relationship with the Lord, I also saw some things that made me go "hmmm":

The more I walk with the Lord, the more I recognize how little I control. I thought my successes and failures depended on me. The truth of the matter is, I tell God my plans, and He blesses them as He sees fit.

The more I will things to happen, the more likely they won't. I recall looking forward to some important celebratory milestones. I did everything humanly possible to ensure that things turned out right. However, when things should have come together, they fell apart. At the appointed time, things worked out better than originally expected! God moved according to His will, not mine.

The more I try to change myself, the more I stay the same. Changing other people is nearly impossible, but changing one's self is challenging, too! As a child I was taught that anything I set my mind to do, I could do. As an adult, though, I know that it takes a lot more than sheer willpower to stop certain behaviors. Real, lasting, transformative change requires Holy Ghost power.

God's vantage point provides a new mindset to see ourselves and our situations through His eyes. It gives us clearer insight and helps us to find our divine purpose. God's perspective takes the focus off of us and places it where it has belonged all the time—on Him.

Lord, we spend a lot of time looking at ourselves through someone else's eyes. Help us to place more emphasis on how You see us, instead of how we see ourselves. In Jesus' name we pray. Amen.

NOT MY WILL, BUT THY WILL BE DONE.

THE LAYOVER

"Dear brothers and sisters, when troubles of any kind come your way, consider it an opportunity for great joy. For you know that when your faith is tested, your endurance has a chance to grow. So let it grow, for when your endurance is fully developed, you will be perfect and complete, needing nothing" (James 1:2–4 NLT).

Traveling to North Carolina for our annual family trip is always a challenge. Since the nine-hour drive is somewhat grueling, one year we decided to fly. We thought that boarding a plane would save time and energy. On the contrary; we were about to encounter a delay of the worst kind.

The plane had mechanical issues that wouldn't be fixed until the following morning. Agonized at the thought of staying overnight in an airport, I prayed for a better solution. Thankfully, God responded quickly. We were given a complimentary hotel room and dinner for the night. Additionally, we were given airline vouchers for a future flight. I was ecstatic, the kids were happy, and my husband was relieved! Early the next morning, we caught our flight and reached our destination with no further problems. It didn't take long to realize that this layover was more of a blessing than a disruption to our plans.

By definition, a layover is a period of rest or waiting before a further stage in a journey. With this resonating thought, I liken the aforementioned layover to my current situation. It began a year ago when I, along with several thousand other employees, was laid off from work due to corporate downsizing. I knew the day was coming; it had been announced three months prior. Yet the weight and finality of it all came crashing down on me like a one-winged 747. How could twenty-six years of loyal service end on such a sour note? I had every reason to believe that retirement was in the not-too-distant future. This devastating loss left me reeling.

As I job hunted in the months that followed, I came to realize that I was in the midst of a real-life layover. I was in a holding pattern.

Unlike the airport experience, this time I had to figure out how to reach my destination (destiny) on my own. I felt alone and lonely, as if stranded on a desert island. Ironically, in this place of darkness was where I began to see God in a whole new light. The light shone so brightly, until I could see a pair of footprints in the sand. That's when I discovered that the Lord had been carrying me the entire time! Overjoyed, I settled in for a safe landing.

There are some roads we must go alone, but because God is on our side, we don't have to bear our burdens alone. Trust Him to work out things in your favor. If you hold on, He'll transform your brokenness for His glory and for your good.

Lord, sometimes You make me wait longer than I'd like, but it's for my good. Thanks for knowing how to take better care of me than I can of myself.

YOU ARE NOW CLEAR FOR TAKE-OFF!

JESUS, TAKE THE WHEEL

"I will instruct you and teach you in the way you should go; I will counsel you with my loving eye on you" (Psalm 32:8 NIV).

Stopped at a red light, a young lady nervously pulled up beside me in a marked driving school car. A male instructor sat calmly on the passenger side. I wondered if his confident demeanor was largely due to the duplicate controls that allowed him to take over in case of an emergency.

This situation mirrors my walk with Christ. He's right by my side when I need him—sometimes reducing my speed when I move too fast, or directing me when I don't know which way to go. And because my safety is His main priority, if the need arises, He simply takes the wheel!

I can recall a time when I was unexpectedly turned in another direction. At first I resisted, because I thought that I knew where I was going. But Jesus saw the danger ahead and forced me off the road.

My abrupt exit came in the form of a massive layoff. I was extremely disappointed. Logic told me to find a job in another division of the company, but it became apparent that God wanted me to pull off that road. He was clearly directing me to go elsewhere.

God has a way of leading us out of life's detours. Instead of doubting Him, try trusting Him. He knows the best route to get us to our divine destinations.

Lord Jesus, forgive me when I question Your will for my life. From now on, I trust You to steer me in the right direction.

LET JESUS TAKE CONTROL. HE KNOWS EXACTLY WHERE YOU'RE GOING.

REST IN PEACE

"Come to me, all you who are weary and burdened, and I will give you rest" (Matthew 11:28 NIV).

"Rest in Peace" is a term generally reserved for the dead. It wishes eternal rest and peace to one who has passed away. Paradoxically, in these polarizing times, I submit that R.I.P. could also be used as a healing salutation for the living.

Today, when you turn on the television or browse social media feeds, you're bound to see vitriol being spewed everywhere. Americans are split along party, racial, and gender lines. People are upset about their present condition and the uncertainty of their children's future. The anguish is palpable, and if this civil unrest continues, our country will suffer grave consequences.

Even so, it's never too late to turn around negativity. A child of God can be a voice of reason and reconciliation. You have the power to shift conversations and restore fellowship in your circles of influence. First, start by answering these questions for yourself: *"Am I contributing to this great divide? Am I killing people with my words or giving life with the Word?"* Introspection is essential to the healing process.

We all want what's best for ourselves, our families, and our country. And of course, God does, too. So if the love of Jesus is in your heart, then share it with others. The proclamation of the Good News, which is the Gospel, gives hope to a dying world. Beloved, all our days are numbered. The day will come when we'll have to exchange our earthly burdens for our heavenly home. In the meantime, let's do our best to rest in peace with one another.

Holy Spirit, we want to lay to rest the petty differences that separate us. Help us to be peacemakers, not dividers. In Jesus' name we pray. Amen.

PEACE BE WITH YOU.

GROWTH SPURTS

"And the boy Samuel continued to grow in stature and in favor with the Lord and with people" (1 Samuel 2:26 NIV).

Anthony Davis was a small, unheralded guard in middle school. At age fifteen, he grew an astounding eight inches in one year, from 6'2" to 6'10". By his senior year of high school, he'd become a highly sought-after college basketball recruit.

The average person will never experience growth of this magnitude, at least not in the natural. However, in the spiritual realm, we all have the capacity to grow to gigantic proportions. In either case, there will be some kind of pain or discomfort.

For a couple of years, I was stretched beyond limits—emotionally, financially, and medically. Some struggles were shared with loved ones; others stayed between me and God. Over time, I realized that He alone had the answers I was seeking. He was the only one who could solve my problems. My faith grew in leaps and bounds as He delivered me from every one of my troubles.

While waiting on the Lord, I learned how to draw strength and comfort from His Word. Most of all, I learned to completely depend on Him to do what I couldn't do for myself. This confidence opened up doors to new hope and possibility for the future.

Most people want to avoid pain at all costs. But when you trust God, your trials won't defeat you; they'll promote you. Children of the Most High God are crowned with favor. Today, Anthony "The Brow" Davis is an NBA All-Star. He's living out his dream, and so am I.

Dear Lord, we will stop murmuring and complaining about our growing pains. While they may not feel good, we know that they work for our good. Thank You for doing what only You can do.

GROWTH SPURTS ACCELERATE THE PROCESS OF MOVING US TO THE NEXT LEVEL.

PROPELLED TO GREATER HEIGHTS

"The Lord is my strength and shield. I trust him with all my heart.
He helps me, and my heart is filled with joy. I burst out in songs of
thanksgiving" (Psalm 28:7 NLT).

Consumed by every issue that surfaced, I was starting to suffocate under the pressure of it all. "Letting go and letting God" was especially difficult for someone like me, who is used to controlling everything and everybody. For one, as a mom, fixing things is par for the course. And two, as the controllership manager of a major corporation, solving problems was literally my job. In other words, controlling things was my thing! Relinquishing control was a huge challenge for me, but I had to find a way.

The hardest part was taming my thoughts and controlling my emotions. As much as I didn't want it to, my overactive mind dictated my moods. There was a clear disconnect between my head and my heart. See, in my head, I wondered where in the world God was in all of this. Yet in my heart, I believed He was right there with me.

Eventually, I learned to bridge the gap through daily worship and fellowship with God. A ritual of praying, meditating, writing, reading, and singing were all settling to my soul. But the real epiphany came when I realized that the joy of the Lord is not about feeling; it's about trusting. I was able to fully release all of my worries and frustrations when I began whole-heartedly trusting God to be my strength and shield.

Beloved, our trials are not meant to take us down; they're designed to raise us up. Ultimately, I discovered that my mounting problems were actual stepping stones that propelled me to greater heights of God's goodness and faithfulness.

Lord, we have our part to play, but we must remember
that You are always in control. Help us to do what we can
and then step aside, so You can do what we cannot.

GOD HAS THE SOLUTION BEFORE WE HAVE
THE PROBLEM.

ON TOP

"But those who hope in the Lord will renew their strength. They will soar on wings like eagles; they will run and not grow weary, they will walk and not be faint" (Isaiah 40:31 NIV).

It can be scary flying in an airplane, especially when you're way above the clouds. There are good reasons, though, why pilots have to fly so high in the sky. For one, the air in the earth's atmosphere becomes thinner as the altitude increases; and two, flying too close to the clouds makes it very hard to see.

Determined to rise above my gloomy circumstances, I made a conscious decision to consider these factors in my own life. I had become painfully aware of my sensibilities and vulnerabilities while going through a very difficult season of change. A job loss, coupled with perceived rejection by others, had clouded my judgement. That is, until a moment of clarity came to me while on a recent flight.

It had been raining on the ground, but once we ascended over the dark clouds, bright sunshine sprang forth! It was dry, beautiful, and clear up near the heavens. I realized then that viewing my life from below only allowed me to see a ceiling of thick, gray clouds. However, at high altitude, above the clouds, I could see God's glory.

The sky painted a vivid picture of what I was doing wrong. I was in a hopeless state because of the limited vision I had for myself, plus the limitations I had placed on God. As I processed this revelation, light filled my weary soul and my burdens began to roll away. I exited the plane with renewed strength and vigor.

I have learned that our trials prepare us for the next level. They take us from glory to glory and from grace to grace. Don't allow hard times to steal your joy. Put your hope in the Lord. He will lift you up when you're down. He will give you courage to overcome your fears. He did it for me, and I believe He's just waiting to do the same for you. The question is: are you ready to f-l-y?

Forgive Others

Let Go

Yield to God

HIGHER IS CALLING! SOAR TO NEW HEIGHTS
WITH CHRIST.

TAKE A LEAP

"And without faith it is impossible to please God, because anyone who comes to him must believe that he exists and that he rewards those who earnestly seek him" (Hebrews 11:6 NIV).

Leap Year usually occurs every four years. The year contains one extra day—366 instead of the normal 365. The last leap year was in 2016. Ironically, that was also the year that I had to take a leap of faith.

At that point, my layoff was imminent. Several rounds had already preceded mine. It was just a matter of time before the next wave. Gloom and doom permeated the office. I had no desire to leave the company before retirement, but it didn't matter now. God had interrupted my plans.

Overwhelmed with uncertainty, I sought Jesus for wisdom and guidance. I needed to understand why this had happened and what I should do next. I partnered in prayer with a good friend and former colleague. We believed God together for direction and provision. As believers, we knew He wouldn't close one door without opening another.

For months and months, we went without securing new jobs. It was hard, but the struggle was not in vain. Losing our jobs led us to make career choices we would not have made otherwise. Stepping out in faith, my friend became an entrepreneur, and I moved from the business world into education and became a writer.

Every now and then, God sends extra trials along to prove His presence in our lives. In these trying times, we must give Him room to turn our obstacles into opportunities. He wouldn't allow the hardships to come if they weren't going to thrust us forward.

Dear Lord, help me to step out in faith when I don't know what to do. I trust You to keep me from falling.

WHEN WE TAKE ONE STEP, GOD TAKES TWO.

BUT GRACE

"But he said to me, 'My grace is sufficient for you, for my power is made perfect in weakness'" (2 Corinthians 12:9 NIV).

After being jolted by yet another sudden change, my normally secure footing landed on shaky ground. I didn't move, for fear of falling. Instead I stood still, waiting for the promises of God to manifest: the trades of joy for my sadness and beauty for my ashes. I held on to the belief that this would come to pass.

For the longest time, though, things remained the same. So much so that I grew weak and despondent. But grace appeared in the nick of time and propped me up on every leaning side. God's grace sustained me. He gave me the strength I needed to endure until the end.

My wilderness experience taught me that change simply means trusting God in a brand-new way. I learned how to set aside my expectations and to believe that His will is far better than my will. Through it all, I discovered that God's grace is at work every day, but it shines the brightest in my darkest hour.

Dear Lord, thank You for being a leaning post when I'm weak. I depend on Your strength and power, especially in times of trouble. I can always count on You.

THE GRACIOUS HAND OF GOD IS UPON ME.

NEW
AND IMPROVED

"And I am certain that God, who began the good work within you,
will continue his work until it is finally finished on the day when
Christ Jesus returns" (Philippians 1:6 NLT).

My circumstances had robbed me of the person I used to be. On the outside I looked the same, but on the inside, something had drastically changed. I didn't know if this was good or bad.

Heartbreaking events completely forced me out of my comfort zone and into unfamiliar territory. I was used to acceptance, but it seemed like rejection was the new order of the day. First my former company, then prospective employers, and now God? I mean, why else couldn't I feel His presence anymore?

Revelation came after much prayer and reflection. God had shifted away from me, so I would have to reposition myself. He was still within my grasp. I just had to try harder and go a little farther to reach Him. I felt like a baby learning how to walk. Initially, I stumbled, but the Lord guided me with His hand. He cheered me on until I had the ability to balance myself and the confidence to take a few steps forward. I'm on the move again, in between where I used to be and where I'm going. On my way to my destiny!

I don't always understand what God does or allows to happen. However, in the case of my layoff, I believe that He took away my job security to show me that He would still provide. He proved to me that the company was a resource, but He is my Source. Today, I am much wiser and stronger because of the journey.

Have you lost connection with your former self? If you answered yes, and have changed into someone you no longer recognize, please don't presume the worst. Instead, beloved, consider this: maybe, just maybe, God is growing you into a new and improved version of yourself.

Lord, You are good! I'm mighty grateful that You're able to love me as I am, while growing me into who You created me to be.

GOD'S TRANSFORMING POWER MOVES US TO THE NEXT LEVEL.

EPILOGUE

Despite the harsh realities of loss, God is still able to mend broken pieces and breathe life into dead situations. Even when we don't feel His presence, we must remember that He is always near. We tend to forget this sometimes, especially when our pain is at its greatest.

Personal storms had blurred my view so badly that I couldn't see what was right in front me. Thankfully, there was a silver lining in the sky. This season taught me how to walk by faith, not by sight. I didn't choose to give up my job. The decision was made for me, and it hurt me to my core. Even so, I wouldn't change what happened, because the loss made room for new opportunities. I was blessed with ample time to complete overdue home projects, to undertake divine assignments, to explore other areas of interest, to enjoy my family, to reunite with old friends, to reconnect with my Creator, and to write this book. Looking back, I can say that the time was well spent.

My life has changed for the better, for several reasons. I am less stressed because I understand that I don't have to figure out, control, or like everything that happens. I appreciate every good day and even the seemingly bad ones. Most of all, I have gained a deeper trust in my Lord.

We all go through difficulties, but no matter the crisis, we must trust the Master's plan. Trust Him when you don't understand; He knows all. Trust Him when times get rough; He will see you through. Trust Him when people reject you; He accepts you as you are. Trust Him when you can't see what lies ahead; He'll guide you. Trust Him when circumstances change; He's doing the repositioning.

I believe that we find the greatest joy and fulfillment when we pursue God's purpose for our lives. The next phase of my life is still unfolding, but I'm waiting patiently, for I know He's working out everything for my good! If you believe like I do, then the same will happen for you... in due time.

ABOUT THE AUTHOR

Ronice Felicia Latta is a former loan accounting manager for GE Capital. She was in a waiting season when she realized that she really wanted to be a writer. This book is her first published work. To those who know her best, Ronice is a woman who is committed to her family, and who wants to make an impact for God's kingdom. She lives in Connecticut with her husband, Lenwood, and their two children, Jalen and Jordan.

CPSIA information can be obtained
at www.ICGtesting.com
Printed in the USA
LVHW100902311219
642042LV00021BB/1499/P